Jeremy Jaguar loved jam.
Jungleberry jam was Jeremy's favorite.

Jeremy loved jam on toast

jam on pancakes

jam on muffins

even jam on ham!

One day, a terrible thing happened.
Jeremy Jaguar ran out of jam!

"I must pick some jungleberries
to make more jam," said Jeremy.
Jeremy waited until the first day of July,
when the jungleberries would be ripe.

Jeremy put on his jersey and jumped
in his jeep. He drove through the jungle
to the place where the jungleberry trees grew.

Soon he saw the trees up ahead.
The jungleberries were as bright as jewels!

As Jeremy got closer to the jungleberry trees,
he heard jazzy music playing.

Jeremy peeked through the bushes.

"Jumping June bugs!" said Jeremy.
"It's a jaguar jamboree!"
Jaguars from every part of the jungle
had come to pick jungleberries.

The jaguars were jumping,
jitterbugging, and jiving.
And best of all,
they were making jam!

Jeremy joined the jamboree.
He jumped. He jitterbugged. He jived.
And he ate jungleberry jam until he thought
he would burst.

When the jamboree was over, Jeremy packed
his jeep with jam jars and drove home.
Now every July, he joins the other jaguars for
the jungleberry jamboree. And the jaguar who
eats the most jam is always Jeremy!

How many things can you find that begin with the letter J?

See inside back cover for answers.

15

Jj Cheer

J is for jaguars, jumping high

J is for jam, jeep, and July

J is for jungle, jug, jar, and jeans

J is for juice and jellybeans

Hooray for J, big and small—

the jazziest, jolliest letter of all!